Where Your Treasure Is

What the Bible Says About Money

JAMES AND MARTHA
REAPSOME

FISHERMAN
BIBLE STUDY SERIES

Where Your Treasure Is
PUBLISHED BY WATERBROOK PRESS
12265 Oracle Boulevard, Suite 200
Colorado Springs, CO 80921
A division of Random House, Inc.

ISBN 0-87788-034-4

Printed in the United States of America
2006

10 9 8 7 6 5 4 3

Contents

How to Use This Studyguide

F isherman studyguides are based on the inductive approach to Bible study. Inductive study is discovery study; we discover what the Bible says as we ask questions about its content and search for answers. This is quite different from the process in which a teacher *tells* a group *about* the Bible—what it means and what to do about it. In inductive study, God speaks directly to each of us through his Word.

A group functions best when a leader keeps the discussion on target, but the leader is neither the teacher nor the "answer person." A leader's responsibility is to *ask*—not *tell*. The answers come from the text itself as group members examine, discuss, and think together about the passage.

There are four kinds of questions in each study. The first is an *approach question*. Asked and answered before the Bible passage is read, this question breaks the ice and helps you start thinking about the topic of the Bible study. It begins to reveal where thoughts and feelings need to be transformed by Scripture.

Some of the earlier questions in each study are *observation questions*—who, what, where, when, and how—designed to help you learn some basic facts about the passage of Scripture.

Once you know what the Bible says, you need to ask, *What does it mean?* These *interpretation questions* help you discover the writer's basic message.

Next come *application questions,* which ask, *What does it mean to me?* They challenge you to live out the Scripture's life-transforming message.

Fisherman studyguides provide spaces between questions for jotting down responses as well as any related questions you would like to raise in the group. Each group member should have a copy of the studyguide and may take a turn in leading the group.

A group should use any accurate, modern translation of the Bible such as the *New International Version,* the *New American Standard Bible,* the *New Living Translation,* the *New Revised Standard Version,* the *New Jerusalem Bible,* or the *Good News Bible.* (Other translations or paraphrases of the Bible may be referred to when additional help is needed.) Bible commentaries should not be brought to a Bible study because they tend to dampen discussion and keep people from thinking for themselves.

Suggestions for Group Leaders

1. Thoroughly read and study the Bible passage before the meeting. Get a firm grasp on its themes and begin applying its teachings for yourself. Pray that the Holy Spirit will "guide you into all truth" (John 16:13) so that your leadership will guide others.

2. If any of the studyguide's questions seem ambiguous or unnatural to you, rephrase them, feeling free to add others that seem necessary to bring out the meaning of a verse.

3. Begin (and end) the study promptly. Start by asking someone to pray that every participant will both understand the passage and be open to its transforming power. Remember, the Holy Spirit is the teacher, not you!

4. Ask for volunteers to read the passages aloud.

5. As you ask the studyguide's questions in sequence, encourage everyone to participate in the discussion. If some are silent, try gently suggesting, "Let's have an answer from someone who hasn't spoken up yet."

6. If a question comes up that you can't answer, don't be afraid to admit that you're baffled. Assign the topic as a research project for someone to report on next week, or say, "I'll do some studying and let you know what I find out."

7. Keep the discussion moving, but be sure it stays focused. Though a certain number of tangents are inevitable, you'll want to quickly bring the discussion back to the topic at hand. Also, learn to pace the discussion so that you finish the lesson in the time allotted.

8. Don't be afraid of silences; some questions take time to answer, and some people need time to gather courage to speak. If silence persists, rephrase your question, but resist the temptation to answer it yourself.

9. If someone comes up with an answer that is clearly illogical or unbiblical, ask for further clarification: "What verse suggests that to you?"

10. Discourage overuse of cross references. Learn all you can from the passage at hand, while selectively incorporating a few important references suggested in the studyguide.

11. Some questions are marked with a *𝄢*. This indicates that further information is available in the Leader's Notes at the back of the guide.

12. For more information on getting a new Bible study group started and keeping it functioning effectively, read *You Can Start a Bible Study Group* by Gladys M. Hunt and *Pilgrims in Progress: Growing Through Groups* by Jim and Carol Plueddemann. (Both books are available from Shaw Books.)

Suggestions for Group Members

1. Learn and apply the following ground rules for effective Bible study. (If new members join the group later, review these guidelines with the whole group.)
2. Remember that your goal is to learn all you can *from the Bible passage being studied.* Let it speak for itself without using Bible commentaries or other Bible passages. There is more than enough in each assigned passage to keep your group productively occupied for one session. Sticking to the passage saves the group from insecurity ("I don't have the right reference books—or the time to read anything else.") and confusion ("Where did *that* come from? I thought we were studying _____.").
3. Avoid the temptation to bring up those fascinating tangents that don't really grow out of the passage you are discussing. If the topic is of common interest, you can bring it up later in informal conversation after the study. Meanwhile, help one another stick to the subject.
4. Encourage one another to participate. People remember best what they discover and verbalize for

themselves. Some people are naturally shy, while others may be afraid of making a mistake. If your discussion is free and friendly and you show real interest in what other group members think and feel, the quieter ones will be more likely to speak up. Remember, the more people involved in a discussion, the richer it will be.

5. Guard yourself from answering too many questions or talking too much. Give others a chance to share their ideas. If you are one who participates easily, discipline yourself by counting to ten before you open your mouth.

6. Make personal, honest applications and commit yourself to letting God's Word change you.

Introduction

S tanding in line for a spaghetti dinner one night, I looked down and spotted a tiny wad of grayish green paper. I picked it up and unfolded it, revealing a one-dollar bill. My young son, who had been standing impatiently beside me, cried, "I saw it first!"

"Ah yes," I replied, "but you didn't think it was worth picking up." His missed chance to make an easy buck grieved him because his pecuniary resources were sparse indeed.

One day I joined a multimillionaire for lunch in Philadelphia, expecting to be treated lavishly. "Let's get some hamburgers," he said. Disappointed, I bleated some weak assent to his absurd proposal. The engagement continued to deteriorate when he asked me to pay for the hamburgers because he didn't have any money. Yet this man lived far above the realm of my son, for whom a dollar bill seemed like a fortune.

Our emotions about money vary as strongly as our feelings about beggars and millionaires because most of us live somewhere between these extremes. Our attitudes about money are largely shaped by our environments and circumstances. Some people make a lot, spend a lot, and have nothing to show for it. Others make a lot, save it, invest it, and accumulate fortunes. Typical wage earners in our society, however, are happy if they can manage to pay for life's necessities, buy a few luxuries, put something aside for their children's educations, and save something for retirement. That's their dream.

Unfortunately, that same cultural dream shapes the attitudes and values of Christians as well—even though they know they are supposed to handle their money differently than the rest of the world. Having spent more than forty years in Christian ministries inside the local church and outside, we believe that Christians suffer from a famine of biblical instruction about money. Even so, they probably spend more time, energy, and thought on money than on any other single aspect of their lives.

We have written this studyguide to end that famine. We believe that Christians want to be biblically informed about all they do—especially about the use of their money—but they don't know where to turn, apart from popular gurus. This book is not a pop guide to wealth. It won't tell you how to budget your income and expenses. But it will give you a solid biblical foundation on which to make those decisions.

The Bible doesn't condemn having wealth, but it does ask how we got it, how important it is to us, and how we use it. This studyguide goes beyond the superficialities and digs for heavy-duty principles we can follow:

- Are we owners or trustees of our possessions?
- How do we know how much is enough?
- Is there a treasure that won't be eaten by inflation?
- How can we control our money and keep our money from controlling us?
- Who determines how much we spend and how much we should give away?
- When all is said and done, can money really buy contentment?

You'll find the answers to these provocative questions not from us, but from your own study of Scripture. Our prayer is that every reader will enjoy the Holy Spirit's enlightenment and come into full obedience to God's will for making, investing, spending, and giving away money.

Possessions: Owner or Trustee?

1 CHRONICLES 29:1-20

A couple was in court making an impassioned plea to the judge. Some money had been left to them in a will, but they argued that the stipulated yearly amount was not enough. The court decided that the money was theirs, though they could not spend it whenever and however they wanted. This was a tough lesson for them to learn.

It's equally difficult for us to learn that everything we have is not really ours, but God's. We are not owners, but trustees. King David recognized this fact as he prepared to build a temple for God. But God gave that task to David's son Solomon. In this passage David assembles the people as he entrusts this task to Solomon and presents his personal gifts for the temple.

1. A friend lets you use his new Lincoln Town Car for a weekend trip. Would you drive and care for

his car differently than you would your own car? Why or why not?

READ 1 CHRONICLES 29:1-9.

✐ 2. How did David demonstrate his devotion to the Lord's temple?

3. What insights into David's heart do you get from his references to the temple as "for the LORD God," "the temple of my God," and "this holy temple" (verses 1-3)?

✐ 4. How had David prepared the way for his direct question in verse 5?

5. What happened in the leaders and the people as a result of their willingness to give themselves to God (verses 6-9)?

Why does giving oneself to God lead to generosity and rejoicing?

READ I CHRONICLES 29:10-20.

✐ 6. David began his prayer with a burst of praise. What reasons did David find for praising God (verses 10-13)?

7. How do you respond to such a description of God?

8. What did David acknowledge about the people and their gifts (verses 14-16)?

9. In what sense have all of your possessions come from God's hand? Why do they belong to God?

10. In what way did David make it clear that God is more concerned with people's hearts and motives than with the size of their offerings (verses 17-19)?

11. What were David's concerns as expressed in the requests he made for the people and Solomon (verses 17-19)?

✐ 12. How would thinking of yourself as a trustee rather than an owner affect your attitude toward your possessions?

✐ *Pray the Bible into Life*

- Thank God that he is the owner and giver of everything you have and need.
- Thank him for what he has entrusted to you.
- Ask God to help you love him with humility and joy.
- Praise God together by reading David's prayer in 1 Chronicles 29:10-13.

Earning: How Much Is Enough?

LUKE 12:13-21; EPHESIANS 4:28

When I was a seminary student in the 1950s, I bought a week's groceries with the ten dollars I earned selling football-game programs on Saturdays. That was enough to live on in those days. Though I earn more than ten dollars a week now, I sometimes wonder if I have enough, especially as I contemplate what living costs will be five and ten years from now. How much will be enough for education, health care, retirement?

Even millionaires worry about such things. A newspaper reporter once asked J. Paul Getty, the oil executive, if his holdings were worth a billion dollars. Getty replied slowly, "I suppose so, but remember, a billion dollars doesn't go as far as it used to."

Jesus told a story about a man who accumulated more than he ever dreamed possible, a man who seemed to have enough. But God's view of wealth and security differs from ours.

1. Do you feel financially "secure" right now? Why or why not?

READ LUKE 12:13-21.

2. What apparent injustice did the rich man ask Jesus to correct (verse 13)?

3. Why do you think Jesus gave him a warning instead (verse 15)?

4. How does Christ's parable illustrate the point that "a man's life does not consist in the abundance of his possessions" (verse 15)?

5. In the parable, how had the man's riches deceived him?

6. What do the pronouns the rich man used indicate about the size of his world (verses 17-19)?

7. Why did God call this man a fool (verse 20)?

8. What could the man have done to become "rich toward God" (verse 21)?

9. In planning and saving for the future, how do you decide how much is enough?

What can you do to keep your "wants" from turning into "needs"?

Read Ephesians 4:28.

10. According to this verse, what is the reason for earning money?

11. If you adopted the motives for earning described in this verse, how would this affect your attitude toward your job? toward what you are earning?

12. How can you assess how much is enough for your needs in light of the physical and spiritual needs of people throughout the world?

Pray the Bible into Life

- Thank God for all the possessions he has entrusted to you.
- Ask God to protect you from finding your security and pleasure in things.
- Confess the ease with which you turn wants into needs.
- Thank God for the Christians around the world who are "rich toward God."

STUDY 3

Payment: Honest Work, Honest Wage

COLOSSIANS 3:22–4:1

When I was a teenager, I had a factory job that was called piecework. One day the owner called me and my pal into his office. Because we were horsing around on the job, he told us that our productivity had not even earned minimum wage. We were not doing honest work; we were costing him money. On the other hand, not all factory owners pay honest wages. Almost every day we hear news about lawsuits concerning unfair labor practices. Honest work and honest wages seem to be in continual dispute. These fights could be avoided if people paid attention to God's rules for both workers and employers.

The apostle Paul wrote in a culture where slavery was accepted. His guidelines for Christian slaves and masters introduced new ideas that elevated slaves and placed startling responsibilities on masters. In this study we'll examine these biblical guidelines in terms of how employees and employers are to relate to one another.

1. What standard do you use to determine whether you are giving your employer an honest day's work? If you are an employer, how do you determine whether you are treating your employees fairly and honestly?

Read Colossians 3:22–4:1.

2. Put in your own words each of the guidelines for slaves and masters.

3. If Paul were writing to our culture, how do you think he would state these guidelines to Christian employers and employees?

4. What is the difference between the two ways of working described in verse 22?

What examples of each motivation have you seen in everyday life?

⚡ 5. Why would obeying "in everything" not apply to any dishonest or unethical policies of an employer (verses 22-25)?

6. How would you handle a request from your boss that you consider unethical?

7. List some of the jobs you do that seem too insignifi-
    cant to matter to God. What dignity does the com-
    mand in verse 23 give even to those tasks?

8. What effect would it have on your attitude or job
    performance to think of yourself as working for the
    Lord rather than for your boss (verses 23-25)?

✐ 9. What warning and encouragement does verse 25
    offer both employees and employers?

10. Of what did Paul remind both slaves and masters
     (3:24; 4:1)?

     How is each statement an appropriate reminder for
     each group?

11. In what ways do these reminders of eternal rewards
     and accountability to God affect your attitude
     toward your work and/or pay (3:24; 4:1)?

Pray the Bible into Life

- Thank God for your ability to earn a living.
- Thank him that you can serve Christ in your work.
- If someone in the group is unemployed, ask God to provide an appropriate job.
- Thank God that he is fair and just, rewarding us without showing favoritism.

Saving: Burglarproof Treasure

MATTHEW 6:19-34

On one of our visits to another country, our hosts entertained us in their comfortable home. Their car, however, had obviously seen its prime many years ago. Because of steep import duties, replacing it would require a long time of saving. Just when they thought they had saved enough, their currency lost one-third of its value. Overnight their dream of buying a new car vanished.

Devaluations, burglaries, droughts, recessions, stock-market crashes, and acts of terrorism are some of the things that threaten our treasures. Jesus praised a man for preparing for possible unemployment. But he warns us against seeking security in what we save or worrying about possible calamities. Jesus' teaching tells us how we can have a treasure guaranteed to be secure.

1. What is the difference between saving for tomorrow and worrying about tomorrow?

Read Matthew 6:19-24.

2. Why did Jesus speak so strongly against storing up treasures on earth (verses 19-21)?

3. In verse 21, Jesus explained the power our treasures have over us. Why do you think he stated this as he did rather than saying, "Where your heart is, there will your treasure be also"?

4. What can you do to store up treasure that will last?

5. Does this passage mean that Christians should not have insurance policies, property, or savings accounts? Why or why not?

6. Between two statements about the power of money in our lives, Jesus spoke of the effect the eye has on the whole body (verses 22-23). In this context of lasting treasure, in what ways might our eyes be full of light? full of darkness?

7. Why is it impossible to serve two masters (verse 24)?

8. In what ways are money and God rivals for our trust and security?

READ MATTHEW 6:25-34.

9. How did Jesus illustrate the futility of worry?

10. In what ways are Christians to differ from unbelievers in their goals and daily activities (verses 31-33)?

11. Jesus does not promise freedom from trouble (verse 34), but what freedoms would a person enjoy who obeys Christ's commands?

12. Reflect on the financial uncertainties in your life today. In view of verse 30, in what ways can your faith help you cope with these concerns?

✐ 13. To help relieve worry, what practical ways would you recommend to control credit-card spending, to limit borrowing, and to save on a regular basis?

Pray the Bible into Life

- Thank God for the opportunity to store up treasure that will last.
- Ask God to help you see where your treasure and your heart really are.
- Confess your worries about…
- Ask for wisdom and faith to manage your money well.

Investing: Risk or Bury?

MATTHEW 25:14-30

When we bought our first house, Jim asked if I wanted a dishwasher. I thought we could continue getting along without one, but when we saw a sale on dishwashers, we decided the time was right. We ordered one for delivery within a week. The next day's mail brought a letter from Latin America Mission about an evangelism program in Honduras that needed funds for training and literature. As we read the letter, we thought about our dishwasher. How many Bibles would our dishwasher buy?

"What would you think about our canceling the order for the dishwasher and giving the money for Honduras?" Jim asked. "That's exactly what I've been thinking," I replied. So each time I washed the dishes, I prayed for Honduras and thanked God for the privilege of investing our dishwasher money to help people come to faith in the Lord Jesus.

Nearly every day we make choices involving the money God has entrusted to us, and we need the Holy Spirit to help us harmonize our choices with God's will. How do we decide how to use the money God has entrusted to us? To get some guidance, consider the story Jesus told about three servants who were responsible for investing the money their master had entrusted to them.

1. What are some things you invest your money in? Why?

READ MATTHEW 25:14-30.

✒ 2. What seems fair in this story? What seems unfair?

✒ 3. Why do you think the master entrusted different amounts to each of the three servants (verses 14-15)?

4. What risks do you think the first two servants might have taken to double what was entrusted to them (verses 16-17)?

5. Compare the master's responses to the servants who brought him ten talents and four talents (verses 19-23). What were they praised for?

What was important to the master?

6. Why did the third servant hide his talent (verses 18,24-25)?

7. How did the servant's view of himself differ from the master's view of him (verses 24-30)?

8. What fears cause you to act like the third servant at times?

9. Although God has entrusted us with different abilities and amounts of resources, why do we have the same accountability to him?

10. The only way to keep something is to use it. What examples of this principle have you seen in action (verse 29)?

11. The master entrusted the servants with money—not to be protected, but to be used for profit. How can you faithfully invest the money, time, and talents God has entrusted to you so they will multiply to God's glory?

Pray the Bible into Life

- Thank God for the resources he has entrusted to you to use.
- Confess any fear or laziness in facing your accountability to God.
- Thank God that he sees and rewards faithfulness.
- Ask for creativity and wisdom in multiplying your resources for him.

Power of Money: Servant or Master?

MARK 10:17-31

Jean Louis Agassiz, the famous professor of zoology at Harvard in the late 1800s, was invited by an academic society to give a lecture. Agassiz refused because lectures like that took too much time from his valuable research and writing. The society persisted, promising a generous honorarium. "That's no inducement to me," Agassiz replied. "I can't afford to waste my time making money."

His answer sounds strange in our culture where making money often takes priority over church and family responsibilities. Money's grip on our lives happens gradually as our spiritual priorities erode. That is why we need the kind of reality check Jesus forced on the wealthy young man who asked for eternal life. In this passage, one of the most provocative in the Bible, we find ways to gain freedom from our slavery to money.

1. With whom do you usually compare your standard of living and giving: the richest family in your community, a celebrity, a poor inner-city family, a Christian family in a developing country, or some other type of family? Why?

Read Mark 10:17-31.

2. Describe the man who approached Jesus (verses 17-22). What did he want?

    In view of verses 17-20, would you like to have this young man as a friend or neighbor? Why or why not?

3. How did Jesus first respond to this seeker (verses 18-19)?

4. What was the one thing this wealthy man lacked (verses 20-21)?

5. What conflicting emotions did both Jesus and the man most likely feel as the man walked away (verses 22-23)?

6. What statement did Jesus repeat to his disciples (verses 23-24)?

What was their reaction?

7. Why do you think it is so hard for a rich person to enter the kingdom of God?

8. What was Peter really asking Jesus by his statement in verse 28?

9. What kinds of wealth did Jesus promise to those who sacrifice for him and the gospel (verses 29-31)?

10. What examples have you seen of these promises being fulfilled?

11. How do you deal with the temptation to put money and possessions ahead of God and people?

12. What recent choices have you made that show the power—or lack of power—of money in your life?

13. To assess the power of money in your life, ask yourself the following questions:

What do I think about when I have nothing else to do?

What do I fret about most?

What is the thing I most dread losing?

Pray the Bible into Life

- Thank Jesus for his loving patience with the rich man, with Peter, and with you.
- Ask God to help you see how much power money has in your life.
- Ask for grace and power to love God and people more than things.
- Praise God that he recognizes and rewards every sacrifice you make for Jesus and the gospel.

Spending: Whose Agenda?

HAGGAI 1; 1 CORINTHIANS 10:23-24

S ociologists say you can determine the values of a culture by looking at the magazine titles on the newsstand. If that's true, then our American culture is enmeshed in sex, beauty, food, sports, travel, and computers. And don't overlook the welter of articles about homes and gardens—everything from adding decks to the latest in interior design and fashions. Our houses occupy our dreams and our daily duties. They also eat up billions of dollars. That's why Christians who want to honor God with their incomes should exercise caution so that even their homes come under Christ's lordship.

One of the most remarkable messages about money and houses comes from a voice out of the past, that of the prophet Haggai. Following their exile to Babylon, the Israelites returned to Jerusalem to rebuild the temple. But the former captives forgot their purpose and settled for life as usual, eking out a

living in a harsh environment. After ten years Haggai arrived
with a message from God.

1. Do you think your Christian neighbors are less spir-
    itual than you are if they have large, beautiful homes
    or luxury cars, and you don't? Why or why not?

READ HAGGAI 1.

   ⟋ 2. What were the main points of the message God
         gave to Haggai (verses 1-11)?

   3. What picture do you get of daily life for these
       returned exiles (verses 5-6,9-11)?

   4. In what ways, if any, do you identify with the
       description of life in verse 6?

5. How did God's agenda and the people's agenda differ (verses 2-4,7-11)?

6. In what different things did God and the people take pleasure (verses 5-9)?

How did the people's goals differ from what God expected of them?

✎ 7. What does your use of time and money during the past week reveal about your real agenda and goals?

8. Why did the leaders and the people respond so promptly to Haggai's message (verses 12-15)?

9. When the people obeyed, God gave them a new message (verse 13). How is this message both appropriate and adequate when we obey him?

10. How do you think Haggai might rephrase his question in verse 4 if he were speaking to us today?

READ 1 CORINTHIANS 10:23-24.

11. In Haggai's warning, God was not condemning the people's having a paneled family room, but rather, he condemned their selfish preoccupation with their own wants and their neglect of him. The New Testament guidelines in 1 Corinthians 10 help us focus on our choices. If all purchases were permissible

and you had the money, how would you decide if the purchase was beneficial? constructive? not just for your own good, but for the good of others?

🖋 12. What practical steps can a Christian family take to set limits on its standard of living? on how much family members spend and for what?

Pray the Bible into Life

- Thank God for his loving reproof when you need it.
- Ask God to help you identify the right priorities for spending and giving.
- Ask God to help you distinguish between what is permissible and what is beneficial and constructive.
- Thank God that self-gratification doesn't satisfy our souls.

Giving: Impulse or Plan?

1 CORINTHIANS 16:1-4; 2 CORINTHIANS 8:1-15

The phone rang one evening, and a polite, cheerful woman greeted Martha. She represented a highly respected mission organization with an urgent need; she asked for one hundred dollars. When Martha explained that we have a plan and budget for our giving, the woman continued to press her case. Martha told her that we do consider and pray about giving to special emergency needs, but that we do not make such decisions on the spot. Could she mail us some information? No, she needed to have our commitment right then. If we couldn't give one hundred dollars, could we at least give twenty-five?

Deciding how and when to give of our resources is difficult. Unfortunately, fund-raising among Christians often looks like high-pressure salesmanship. Faced with these pressures, many Christians either get angry or give out of compulsion. The Bible spells out a better way to ask and to give.

1. Why do you think some Christians resist the idea of making financial pledges to the church or to missions even though they do not seem to feel bothered by home mortgages or installment buying?

Read 1 Corinthians 16:1-4.

2. What general guidelines about giving do you find in this passage?

3. Look more carefully at verse 2. Why do you think Paul gave instructions for planned giving as a part of weekly worship for every Christian, regardless of his or her income?

4. Paul was careful to ensure accountability in the delivery of the gift to Jerusalem. How can you

ensure that your own financial gifts are handled responsibly and with accountability?

READ 2 CORINTHIANS 8:1-15.

5. What factors made the Macedonians' giving commendable (verses 1-5)?

6. Paul described giving as "this act of grace" (verse 6) and as "this grace of giving" (verse 7). How is giving an act of grace?

7. In what ways is the Lord Jesus our model for giving (verse 9)?

8. Study verses 10-15. In their desire to help the Christians in Jerusalem, the believers in the Corinthian church had started a fund a year earlier. Now it was time to complete the offering. Why is the acceptable amount of a gift determined by what we *have* rather than by what we *don't have?*

9. Look more carefully at verses 13-15. How might practicing the principle of equality affect the way your church determines its annual budget?

What impact could the teachings of verses 13-15 have on planning your personal budget?

10. Paul made no apology for talking about specific needs and the church's financial responsibility to other Christians in need. How does his appeal differ from the appeals you receive in letters, on television, or from your church (verses 1-15)?

11. How could a plan for giving help you follow the examples of the early church and of Christ himself?

⌐ 12.   In what ways can the system of giving described in
1 and 2 Corinthians help you make decisions about
the various appeals for funds that you receive?

Pray the Bible into Life

- Thank God for the grace of giving seen in the Lord
  Jesus, in churches, and in individuals you know.
- Ask God to help you see giving as a privilege and a
  spiritual gift.
- Confess your fear or reluctance to give of yourself—
  and your wallet—to God.
- Pray for wisdom and accountability for Christian
  leaders who must administer funds responsibly.

Generosity: Gracious Giving

2 CORINTHIANS 9:6-15

A friend of ours was trying to teach his grandson about regular giving to God. After they returned from the recycling truck where Jonathan had earned $17, Grandfather helped him figure out what 10 percent—a tithe—of $17 would be. As Jonathan deposited $1.70 in his "Jesus Bank," he proudly declared, "Look how much I gave to Jesus!" "Yes, but look how much you have left for Jonathan," responded Grandfather.

Too often, it seems, we feel that after we've put our offering in the plate and sent off our check to the mission board our job for God is done. We smile with a sense of smug relief, knowing that we have a lot more left for ourselves than we've given to God. But we've learned in this study that nothing is ours; God is the owner of all we have. That truth is the foundation of Christian stewardship. The apostle Paul went a step further and said that because Jesus gave everything, so should we. But how? This study is a guide to generous and gracious giving.

1. Dr. Lyle Schaller of Yokefellow Institute says that in churches with many marginal members, only 20 percent of the people pay 80 percent of the budget. Even in the typical church, one-third of the people pay for two-thirds of the budget. Why do you think this happens?

   How or when did you first learn that giving could make you happy?

READ 2 CORINTHIANS 9:6-15.

2. As Paul continued to instruct the early church in Corinth about giving, what guidelines did he add in verses 6 and 7?

3. What are the purposes of God's blessings—for the giver and for others (verses 8-11)?

Which of these purposes is being fulfilled in your own life? Explain.

4. How does the promise in verse 8 address our fears about generous giving?

⌀ How does this promise differ from the popular idea that we should give so that we ourselves can get rich?

5. According to verses 10 and 11, what needs will God provide for? To what end?

✍ 6. What do you think it means to have a "harvest of…righteousness" and to be "made rich in every way" (verses 10-11)?

✍ 7. How has God enriched your life or your church through someone else's giving? (Consider the gifts of time and abilities as well as money.)

8. Look more carefully at verses 12-15. How does generous giving multiply thanks and prayers to God?

9. In what ways did Paul show that the source of generous giving is our heart of faith, not our wallets?

10. Why did Paul conclude his plea for generous giving with "Thanks be to God for his indescribable gift" (verse 15)?

11. How would Paul's message encourage the Christian who has little to give?

12. What is the overall tone of Paul's teaching on the grace of giving?

How does your approach to giving compare with Paul's approach? What can you do to become more like the kind of giver Paul described?

Pray the Bible into Life

- Think of words you can use to describe God's "indescribable gift," the Lord Jesus, and thank God for his gift.
- Thank God for his generous grace that allows you to do "every good work" and to increase in righteousness.

- Thank God for particular people who have been generous to you with their money, time, or love.
- Ask God to help you become a more cheerful, generous giver.

How Do You Spell *Contentment?*

I Timothy 6:6-10,17-19

B ing Crosby, the popular American singer and actor, was once asked why he had such a calm, unruffled air. He reached into his pocket and pulled out an enormous wad of bills. "That helps!" he said. Many people seek security and contentment in money, and money magazines oblige by telling us how to achieve so-called financial security. Beyond the money itself, of course, lies the hope of contentment and freedom from anxiety, especially in old age.

The ancient Roman world also felt that money brought security and contentment. With the gospel of Jesus Christ, however, came a revolutionary idea: Through Christ you can achieve contentment without necessarily having lots of money. In this study the apostle Paul expounds upon this radical concept. He does not criticize money itself, but he does force us to look at the deepest roots of our desires.

1. When you were growing up, what did money mean to your parents (i.e., status, power, a means to an end, or something else)?

✐ READ 1 TIMOTHY 6:6-10.

2. What contrasts did Paul make between contented people and those who want to get rich?

✐ 3. How would you describe the "great gain" that comes to contented, godly people (verse 6)?

⌁ 4. What perspective did Paul give as a basis for contentment (verses 7-8)?

What are some ways you can learn to be content after your basic needs are met?

5. According to Paul, money itself is not a problem, but the desire to get rich or the love of money is. In what ways, if any, have these desires been a trap for you or for people you know?

6. What will result from greed (verses 9-10)?

READ 1 TIMOTHY 6:17-19.

7. According to these verses, what did Paul command the rich to do and not do?

8. The church in North America enjoys unprecedented wealth. If you applied these verses to yourself and to your church, what difference would they make?

9. In view of the danger of riches, why do you think Paul did not command the rich to sell everything they have and give to the poor?

10. How could verse 17 free you from worrying about not having what you need?

How could it free you from guilt about enjoying what God gives you?

↗ 11. In view of verses 18 and 19, what steps can you take to lay up true riches now and for the future?

12. Reflect on the Bible's overall teaching about the place of money in your life. What principles will guide you in making future decisions about how you earn and use God's money?

Pray the Bible into Life

- Thank God for all he has richly given you to enjoy.
- Ask for help to resist cultural attitudes toward money that would lead you to make accumulating money your goal.
- Ask God to teach you contentment. Thank him that this quality can be learned.
- Ask for grace to obey the commands in these studies.

Leader's Notes

STUDY 1: POSSESSIONS

Question 2. Use this question to help your group pick through all of the details in verses 1-5. Be sure the group observes that David gave both from the national resources he had accumulated (verse 2) and from his personal treasures (verses 3-4).

Question 4. Other translations of the question in verse 5 include: "Who then will offer willingly, consecrating himself today to the LORD?" (RSV); "Now who is willing to give with open hand to the LORD today?" (NEB). *Consecrate* means "to set apart" or "to dedicate" to the service of God.

Question 6. Consider the meaning and implications of the words describing God and what he gives. For example, "God of our father Israel" (verse 10), which refers to human history, contrasts with "from everlasting to everlasting" (verse 10), which speaks of God as outside of time. Use the dictionary to help your group define *glory, majesty,* and *splendor* (verse 11). Help people note the scope of God's ownership and authority expressed in verses 11 and 12. People should find at least three things God gives (verse 12).

Question 10. David referred to God as "God of our fathers Abraham, Isaac and Israel" (verse 18). *Abraham* was the man God chose to be the father of the Jewish nation (Genesis 12:1-7). *Isaac* was his son, born when Abraham and his wife, Sarah, were old (Genesis 21:1-5). *Israel,* also named Jacob, was one of the twin sons born to Isaac (Genesis 25:19-26). Israel's sons and their descendants became known as the twelve tribes of Israel.

Question 12. A trustee is a person to whom another's property or the management of another's property is entrusted. The owner's wishes and character affect how the trustee cares for the property. A trustee is accountable to the owner for how the property is used.

Pray the Bible into Life. The leader may direct prayer by reading the prayer suggestions to the group and allowing time for silent or oral sentence prayers; volunteers may choose one item for oral prayer; or several people may offer sentence prayers about any of the suggestions.

Study 2: Earning

Question 5. A false sense of security and temporary delights insulated the rich fool from God. In Mark 4:19 Jesus compared the deceitfulness of wealth to thorns that choke out the Word of God in our lives.

Question 6. The man used the word *I* six times and *my/myself* five times. Note also that he used no pronouns referring to anyone else.

Question 7. The Bible does not condemn having wealth, but loving or trusting wealth and using it selfishly. According to Psalm 14:1, a fool is one who says, "There is no God."

Question 9. The point here is not to create guilt, but to apply Jesus' warning: "Be on your guard against all kinds of greed; a man's life does not consist in the abundance of his possessions" (verse 15).

To gain perspective on our wealth, consider a definition of the poor as "those who have no choices," then list some of the choices we make in a day about what to wear, what to eat, where and how to travel, what to read, what to buy, and so on. Encourage honest discussion of the struggles against rationalizing wants and placing security in our savings and investments.

Question 10. The New Testament cuts across cultures to give a totally new reason to work. Read 2 Thessalonians 3:6-13 and 1 Timothy 5:4,8 for other biblical reasons to earn money.

Question 12. Encourage the group toward larger, global thinking. If the group is not aware of global needs, individuals might volunteer to get information from churches, relief and mission organizations, or missionary friends. Take time before the next study to report to the group.

STUDY 3: PAYMENT

Question 3. Although employers and employees are not exact parallels of masters and slaves, Paul's principles of conduct in this type of relationship are applicable. Paul spoke to a common social structure (slavery) and showed how the gospel made it bearable and how Christians could bear witness to their reverence for Christ even though they were slaves.

Question 5. We are commanded to obey God's laws supremely. His laws countermand laws dictated by earthly masters. The apostles said we must obey God, not men, in such circumstances (Acts 4:18-20).

Question 9. Colossians 3:25 comes before masters are addressed, but it clearly applies to them as well as to slaves. If needed, you may want to ask the group, "Why is God's lack of favoritism a warning?" and "Why is it an encouragement?"

STUDY 4: SAVING

Question 5. People may have different opinions on these issues. Encourage the group to listen carefully to the reasons for each point of view. The goal is not for everyone to agree, but for everyone to understand the issues involved and then make up his or her own mind.

Question 6. The eye, just a small part, influences the whole body. So our generous or grudging attitudes toward money and possessions affect our whole life. The eye can be the gate for the temptation of coveting or greed.

Question 7. Matthew 6:24 could be more accurately translated: "No man can be a slave to two owners." A slave had no time of his own. He lived to serve his master, who had absolute ownership (from William Barclay, *Daily Study Bible, The Gospel of Matthew,* vol. 1, Philadelphia: Westminster, 1958, p. 251).

Question 9. Jesus addressed the basic worries of the ordinary people of his day—many of whom were poor. They lived day to day without any reserves or welfare programs. He pointed them to things they could see as evidences of God's care. He argued from the lesser (birds, flowers) to the greater (their personal survival).

Question 11. Encourage the group to reflect on each command in this study and consider how it offers freedom. Commands appear in Matthew 6:19-20,25,28,31,33.

Question 13. Some in the group may be able to give practical help to other members who may be struggling with financial management. For additional information, see the resource list on page 77.

STUDY 5: INVESTING

Question 2. Jesus told many stories—or parables—to clarify truths. These parables were easily understood because people could identify with them. They are not to be pressed for more than one main point.

Question 3. A talent was not a coin, but a weight of copper, gold, or silver. One talent was equivalent to about sixty-six pounds. The value varied according to the metal involved. A talent was worth more than a thousand dollars, but its value varied according to its composition (from J. D. Douglas, ed., *The New Bible Dictionary,* Grand Rapids: Eerdmans, 1965, pp. 130, 1323).

Question 5. God values faithfulness, not competition and status. Two of the servants proved faithful by doubling the amount the master entrusted to them. We may have differing amounts of resources, but we are equally accountable for using what we have. You might want to ask the group what difference it would have made if the master had said "good and skillful" or "good and hard working" or "good and successful" servant.

Question 8. A person may be tempted to think, *I have so little; what could I do? It's not worth the risk and effort to try.* Fear and a low view of his options led the third servant to hide his resources rather than to invest what the master had entrusted to him. Ask for other reasons why people are afraid to take risks.

Study 6: Power of Money

Question 2. The man obviously was both wealthy and morally upright. We picture him as a devout Jew who knew and kept the laws of Moses. We also gather that he was sincere in raising a question that revealed his spiritual hunger. Apparently, the man thought there was something he could *do* to inherit eternal life. In the Gospels, inheriting eternal life is synonymous with entering the kingdom of God.

Question 3. Jesus raised the issue of who is truly good. Was Jesus forcing the young man to contrast his goodness as a moral person to the true goodness of God? See Exodus 20:1-17 for the "commandments" to which Jesus was referring. The first four commands concern our relationship to God, and the rest concern our relationship to other people. It is interesting that Jesus began his recitation of the commandments with the second tier.

Question 4. This is the only person Jesus told to sell everything. When Zacchaeus, the dishonest tax collector, met Jesus, Zacchaeus promised to make restitution to people he had cheated. Jesus commended him and did not ask him to sell everything (Luke 19:8-9). When wealthy Nicodemus visited him, Jesus talked about being born again, but he never mentioned money (John 3:1-21). Wealthy women followed Jesus and used their wealth to provide for him and his disciples (Mark 15:40-41). Jesus identifies the things or issues in our lives that are more important to us than God is, the things we cherish or trust more than God.

Question 5. Jesus knew this particular young man better than we do. "Jesus…loved him" (verse 21), but Jesus still made this heavy demand of him.

Question 6. Even though the disciples had lived with Jesus for almost three years, they were amazed at his statements in Mark 10:23-25. The Jews of that day believed that material prosperity was evidence of God's blessing and approval. Jesus used hyperbole to illustrate how hard it is for the rich to enter the kingdom of God. It is not just hard, but impossible—as impossible as a camel's going through the eye of a needle. But God, who does the impossible, can save the person who denounces self-sufficiency and trust in money—no matter how much or how little we have.

STUDY 7: SPENDING

Question 2. To understand the setting of Haggai's message, you may want to give the group some background information. In 586 B.C. the Babylonians destroyed the temple in Jerusalem and took the Jews into captivity. After seventy years of exile, some of the survivors had returned to Jerusalem to repair the temple. But after six years of opposition and threats from their enemies, work on the temple had come to a halt.

Question 7. Good intentions and emotions are not accurate measures of what is important to us. Reflecting on how we spend our time and money may reveal a surprising set of priorities.

Questions 11 and 12. The immediate context of 1 Corinthians was a debate about whether Christians could eat meat that had been offered to idols. Paul avoided a legalist prohibition against eating any kind of food. The issue was not whether eating the meat was permissible, but rather what constructive or destructive effect it would have on others—both Christians and nonbelievers. The ideas that are expressed in these final two questions may be new and shocking to some in the group. Encourage honesty in considering ideas that go against our culture.

Study 8: Giving

Question 2. In the early church, giving was part of regular worship on the first day of the week. By then Christians had begun to worship God on Sunday instead of Saturday because Jesus had risen from the dead on a Sunday. Each person was encouraged to regularly set aside money to give, an amount proportional to his or her income. Doing this ensured the funds would be ready when the time came to collect them. A first-century famine in Judea prompted the churches in Greece to establish a relief fund. These churches were instructed to choose trustworthy leaders who would oversee the funds and be held accountable for them. These guidelines for giving are also applicable for the church today. Wherever possible, personal relationships should be part of our giving.

Question 4. Church leaders are accountable for accounting, the proper use of funds, and reports to the congregation. Shared responsibility is a safeguard against one person's misuse of funds as well as the temptation toward personal gain.

The reliability of other charities can be established by asking appropriate questions about outside audits, IRS standing, and membership in such organizations as the Evangelical Council for Financial Accountability, the Evangelical Fellowship of Mission Agencies, and the Interdenominational Foreign Mission Association.

Question 6. The Corinthian church delighted in having all the spiritual gifts. (Paul listed these gifts in Romans 12:5-8 and 1 Corinthians 12:7-11.) Being able to give to God and others is one of the gifts that flow from God's grace. Help your group discuss the relationship between grace and giving as group members attempt to understand these terms.

Questions 11 and 12. At present, the church in North America enjoys unprecedented prosperity while churches in some countries have little or no Christian literature and few trained pastors. Learning how to be partners with believers in these other countries (without creating dependency) requires prayer and wisdom in applying the principle of equality.

STUDY 9: GENEROSITY

Question 4. "Prosperity theology" teaches that if you give generously and sacrificially, God will make you rich, happy, and healthy. With prosperity theology, the motive for giving is to get rich, which is very different from what Paul is saying in this passage. Help your group to explore these opposite motives for giving. Encourage people to cite examples of each.

Questions 6 and 7. A "harvest of righteousness" comes to those who sow their money in the lives of others through their generous gifts. The miracle of food production is duplicated by the miracle of a spiritual harvest. The process with your money is this: God supplies it and then multiplies it when it is given away—not in terms of actual cash, but in terms of spiritual profit. Money given away according to God's will multiplies our efforts toward what is right. Besides, generous Christians are stronger, happier, and more content than those who are stingy.

Question 8. Paul gave two reasons for thanksgiving: the Corinthian's obedience and their generosity. The overflowing praise came from those who benefited from their gifts.

Question 9. The Corinthian Christians responded to the gospel of Christ by faith. Their generous gift for the Christians suffering from famine flowed from their obedience to the Lord Jesus. Paul commended the Macedonian (Greek) Christians for giving themselves first to God and then giving their gifts to help the Jewish Christians in Jerusalem (2 Corinthians 8:5). Their love for God and gratitude for Jesus Christ overcame the social and cultural barriers that would have separated them from the believers in Jerusalem. The issue is our response to the good news of Jesus. All obedience, including generous giving, flows from that commitment. Encourage your group to look first at verse 13, then study the source of giving throughout the passage.

Question 10. The Lord Jesus is God's "indescribable gift" (NIV); "his gift beyond words" (NEB); "his inexpressible gift" (RSV); "his priceless gift" (TEV); "his indescribable generosity to you" (PHILLIPS). If your group needs additional information about the gift of salvation through Jesus Christ, point them to John 3:16 and Romans 5:15-16.

STUDY 10: HOW DO YOU SPELL *CONTENTMENT*?

Read 1 Timothy 6:6-10. Paul's letter to Timothy was packed with practical advice for a new, younger church leader. He wanted his protégé to learn the real secret of joy in ministry because cult leaders and false teachers of his day were flaunting their wealth.

Question 3. Paul contrasted the gains of wealth and the gains of living by faith. The unseen wealth of faith, trust, hope, joy, and peace far outweighs anything represented by financial wealth.

Question 4. Our culture values money and material goods as evidence of success and a person's value. The biblical idea of contentment opposes our culture as well as our selfish nature.

Question 9. Encourage your group to examine the text for potential reasons. People may wonder about the contrast between

Paul's instructions here with Christ's instruction to the rich man in Mark 10. If so, review study 6.

Question 10. Jesus taught that God is a loving Father who provides for his children and delights to give them good gifts (Matthew 6:25-34). Christians can live free of anxiety and greed. God's abundant provisions sometimes surprise us. Since God's gifts are to be *enjoyed,* we don't need to feel guilty for the comfort and beauty God allows us to have.

Question 11. Paul's life reflected what Jesus taught. Contentment, freedom from anxiety, and God's commendation come to those who use earthly treasure to lay up eternal treasure. "So we fix our eyes not on what is seen, but on what is unseen. For what is seen is temporary, but what is unseen is eternal" (2 Corinthians 4:18).

For Further Reading

Alcorn, Randy C. *Money, Possessions, and Eternity,* Rev. ed. Wheaton, Ill.: Tyndale, 2003.

Bates, Judy Woodward. *The Gospel Truth About Money Management.* New Hope, Minn.: New Hope, 2003.

Blanchard, Ken, and S. Truett Cathy. *The Generosity Factor.* Grand Rapids: Zondervan, 2002.

Blue, Ron. *Generous Living.* Grand Rapids: Zondervan, 1997.

Burkett, Larry, and Rick Osborne. *Financial Parenting.* Colorado Springs: Cook, Victor, 1996.

———. *How to Manage Your Money Workbook,* Rev. ed. Chicago: Moody, 2000.

———. *Money Matters.* Nashville: Nelson, 2001.

———. *More Than Finances.* Chicago: Moody, 2000.

Larson, Dale, and Sandy Larson. *How to Spend Less and Enjoy it More.* Wheaton, Ill.: InterVarsity, 1994.

Tuma, Jerry, Ramona Tuma, and Tim LaHaye. *Smart Money.* Sisters, Oreg.: Multnomah, 1994.

Willmer, Wesley K. *God and Your Stuff.* Colorado Springs: NavPress, 2002.

Wood, William C. *Getting a Grip on Your Money.* Wheaton, Ill.: InterVarsity, 2002.

What Should We Study Next?

If you enjoyed this Fisherman Bible Studyguide, you might want to explore our full line of Fisherman Resources and Bible Studyguides. The following books offer time-tested Fisherman inductive Bible studies for individuals or groups.

FISHERMAN RESOURCES

The Art of Spiritual Listening: Responding to God's Voice Amid the Noise of Life by Alice Fryling

Balm in Gilead by Dudley Delffs

The Essential Bible Guide by Whitney T. Kuniholm

Questions from the God Who Needs No Answers: What Is He Really Asking of You? by Carolyn and Craig Williford

Reckless Faith: Living Passionately as Imperfect Christians by Jo Kadlecek

Soul Strength: Spiritual Courage for the Battles of Life by Pam Lau

FISHERMAN BIBLE STUDYGUIDES

Topical Studies

Angels by Vinita Hampton Wright

Becoming Women of Purpose by Ruth Haley Barton

Building Your House on the Lord: A Firm Foundation for Family Life (Revised Edition) by Steve and Dee Brestin

Discipleship: The Growing Christian's Lifestyle by James and
    Martha Reapsome
*Doing Justice, Showing Mercy: Christian Action in Today's
    World* by Vinita Hampton Wright
Encouraging Others: Biblical Models for Caring by Lin Johnson
The End Times: Discovering What the Bible Says by E. Michael
    Rusten
Examining the Claims of Jesus by Dee Brestin
Friendship: Portraits in God's Family Album by Steve and Dee
    Brestin
The Fruit of the Spirit: Growing in Christian Character by
    Stuart Briscoe
Great Doctrines of the Bible by Stephen Board
Great Passages of the Bible by Carol Plueddemann
Great Prayers of the Bible by Carol Plueddemann
Growing Through Life's Challenges by James and Martha
    Reapsome
Guidance & God's Will by Tom and Joan Stark
Heart Renewal: Finding Spiritual Refreshment by Ruth Goring
Higher Ground: Steps Toward Christian Maturity by Steve and
    Dee Brestin
Images of Redemption: God's Unfolding Plan Through the Bible
    by Ruth E. Van Reken
Integrity: Character from the Inside Out by Ted W. Engstrom
    and Robert C. Larson
Lifestyle Priorities by John White
Marriage: Learning from Couples in Scripture by R. Paul and
    Gail Stevens
Miracles by Robbie Castleman
One Body, One Spirit: Building Relationships in the Church by
    Dale and Sandy Larsen

The Parables of Jesus by Gladys Hunt

Parenting with Purpose and Grace by Alice Fryling

Prayer: Discovering What Scripture Says by Timothy Jones and
     Jill Zook-Jones

The Prophets: God's Truth Tellers by Vinita Hampton Wright

Proverbs and Parables: God's Wisdom for Living by Dee Brestin

Satisfying Work: Christian Living from Nine to Five by R. Paul
     Stevens and Gerry Schoberg

Senior Saints: Growing Older in God's Family by James and
     Martha Reapsome

The Sermon on the Mount: The God Who Understands Me by
     Gladys M. Hunt

Speaking Wisely: Exploring the Power of Words by Poppy Smith

Spiritual Disciplines: The Tasks of a Joyful Life by Larry Sibley

Spiritual Gifts by Karen Dockrey

Spiritual Hunger: Filling Your Deepest Longings by Jim and
     Carol Plueddemann

A Spiritual Legacy: Faith for the Next Generation by Chuck
     and Winnie Christensen

Spiritual Warfare by A. Scott Moreau

The Ten Commandments: God's Rules for Living by Stuart
     Briscoe

Ultimate Hope for Changing Times by Dale and Sandy Larsen

When Faith Is All You Have: A Study of Hebrews 11 by Ruth
     E. Van Reken

Where Your Treasure Is: What the Bible Says About Money by
     James and Martha Reapsome

Who Is God? by David P. Seemuth

Who Is Jesus? In His Own Words by Ruth E. Van Reken

Who Is the Holy Spirit? by Barbara H. Knuckles and Ruth
     E. Van Reken

Wisdom for Today's Woman: Insights from Esther by Poppy
    Smith
Witnesses to All the World: God's Heart for the Nations by Jim
    and Carol Plueddemann
Women at Midlife: Embracing the Challenges by Jeanie Miley
Worship: Discovering What Scripture Says by Larry Sibley

Bible Book Studies
Genesis: Walking with God by Margaret Fromer and Sharrel
    Keyes
Exodus: God Our Deliverer by Dale and Sandy Larsen
Ruth: Relationships That Bring Life by Ruth Haley Barton
Ezra and Nehemiah: A Time to Rebuild by James Reapsome
(For Esther, see Topical Studies, *Wisdom for Today's Woman*)
Job: Trusting Through Trials by Ron Klug
Psalms: A Guide to Prayer and Praise by Ron Klug
Proverbs: Wisdom That Works by Vinita Hampton Wright
Ecclesiastes: A Time for Everything by Stephen Board
Song of Songs: A Dialogue of Intimacy by James Reapsome
Jeremiah: The Man and His Message by James Reapsome
Jonah, Habakkuk, and Malachi: Living Responsibly by Mar-
    garet Fromer and Sharrel Keyes
Matthew: People of the Kingdom by Larry Sibley
Mark: God in Action by Chuck and Winnie Christensen
Luke: Following Jesus by Sharrel Keyes
John: The Living Word by Whitney Kuniholm
Acts 1–12: God Moves in the Early Church by Chuck and
    Winnie Christensen
Acts 13–28, see *Paul* under Character Studies
Romans: The Christian Story by James Reapsome

1 Corinthians: Problems and Solutions in a Growing Church
by Charles and Ann Hummel
Strengthened to Serve: 2 Corinthians by Jim and Carol
Plueddemann
Galatians, Titus, and Philemon: Freedom in Christ by Whitney
Kuniholm
Ephesians: Living in God's Household by Robert Baylis
Philippians: God's Guide to Joy by Ron Klug
Colossians: Focus on Christ by Luci Shaw
Letters to the Thessalonians by Margaret Fromer and Sharrel
Keyes
Letters to Timothy: Discipleship in Action by Margaret Fromer
and Sharrel Keyes
Hebrews: Foundations for Faith by Gladys Hunt
James: Faith in Action by Chuck and Winnie Christensen
1 and 2 Peter, Jude: Called for a Purpose by Steve and Dee
Brestin
1, 2, 3 John: How Should a Christian Live? by Dee Brestin
Revelation: The Lamb Who Is the Lion by Gladys Hunt

Bible Character Studies
Abraham: Model of Faith by James Reapsome
David: Man After God's Own Heart by Robbie Castleman
Elijah: Obedience in a Threatening World by Robbie
Castleman
Great People of the Bible by Carol Plueddemann
King David: Trusting God for a Lifetime by Robbie
Castleman
Men Like Us: Ordinary Men, Extraordinary God by Paul
Heidebrecht and Ted Scheuermann

Moses: Encountering God by Greg Asimakoupoulos

Paul: Thirteenth Apostle (Acts 13–28) by Chuck and Winnie
Christensen

Women Like Us: Wisdom for Today's Issues by Ruth Haley
Barton

Women Who Achieved for God by Winnie Christensen

Women Who Believed God by Winnie Christensen